What's the Difference?
Crocodiles and Alligators

by Lisa M. Herrington

Content Consultant

Dr. Lucy Spelman

Reading Consultant

Jeanne M. Clidas, Ph.D.
Reading Specialist

Children's Press®
An Imprint of Scholastic Inc.

Library of Congress Cataloging-in-Publication Data

Herrington, Lisa M., author.
  Crocodiles and alligators / by Lisa M. Herrington.
     pages cm. -- (Rookie read-about science. What's the difference)
  Summary: "Introduces the reader to crocodiles and alligators."-- Provided by publisher.
  ISBN 978-0-531-21483-1 (library binding) -- ISBN 978-0-531-21531-9 (pbk.)
  1. Crocodiles--Miscellanea--Juvenile literature. 2. Alligators--Miscellanea--Juvenile literature. 3. Children's
questions and answers. I. Title.

  QL666.C925H47 2016
  597.98--dc23   2015017323

Produced by Spooky Cheetah Press
Design by Keith Plechaty

© 2016 by Scholastic Inc.

Printed in China 62

SCHOLASTIC, CHILDREN'S PRESS, ROOKIE READ-ABOUT®, and associated logos are trademarks and/or
registered trademarks of Scholastic Inc.

1 2 3 4 5 6 7 8 9 10 R 25 24 23 22 21 20 19 18 17 16

Photographs ©: cover left: McPhoto/age fotostock; cover right: NHPA/Superstock, Inc.; 3 top left:
mezzotint/Shutterstock, Inc.; 3 top right: Bunwit Unseree/Alamy Images; 4 top: nattanan726/Shutterstock,
Inc.; 4 bottom: blickwinkel/Alamy Images; 7 top: nattanan726/Shutterstock, Inc.; 7 bottom: blickwinkel/
Alamy; 8 main: Jason Edwards/Media Bakery; 8 inset: Denis-Huot/Nature Picture Library; 11 main: Ugo
Mellone/Media Bakery; 11 inset: Steven Widoff/Alamy Images; 12: Maximilian Weinzierl/Alamy Images; 15:
TraceRouda/iStockphoto; 16: Rolf Nussbaumer/Nature Picture Library; 19: Hedrus/Shutterstock, Inc.; 20:
Anup Shah/Nature Picture Library; 23: Animals Animals/Superstock, Inc.; 24 left: nattanan726/Shutterstock,
Inc.; 24 right: blickwinkel/Alamy Images; 25 right: Sergey Lavrentev/Shutterstock, Inc.; 25 left: Anup Shah/
Nature Picture Library; 26: Minden Pictures/Superstock, Inc.; 27: blickwinkel/Alamy Images; 28: Raúl Martín;
29: Dan Dry; 30: Tier und Naturfotografie/Superstock, Inc.; 31 top: Hedrus/Shutterstock, Inc.; 31 center top:
Maximilian Weinzierl/Alamy Images; 31 center bottom: Tier und Naturfotografie/Superstock, Inc.; 31 bottom:
Jason Edwards/Media Bakery.

Map by XNR Productions, Inc.

Table of Contents

4

Which Is Which?

They are both fierce hunters. They have sharp teeth and huge jaws. They are **reptiles**, so they have **scaly** skin. They both have powerful tails for swimming. They live in water and on land. But which is the crocodile and which is the alligator?

Did you guess right? Crocodiles and alligators are a lot alike. But they are not exactly the same. There are ways to tell them apart.

Reptiles are cold-blooded. They lie in the sun to warm up—and to digest their meals.

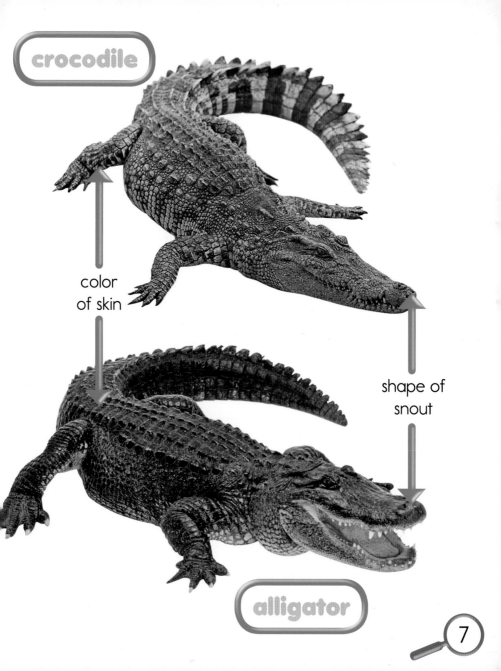

crocodile

color
of skin

shape of
snout

alligator

7

V-shaped snout

The Secret of the Snouts

What is one easy way to tell these animals apart? Look at the shape of their heads.

A crocodile has a long, pointed **snout**. It is shaped like the letter V. When a crocodile closes its mouth, both its top and bottom teeth show.

An alligator has a wide, rounded snout. It is shaped like the letter U. When an alligator closes its mouth, only its top teeth show.

FUN FACT!

Crocodiles and alligators have up to 110 teeth. They often lose their teeth. But new ones grow in quickly.

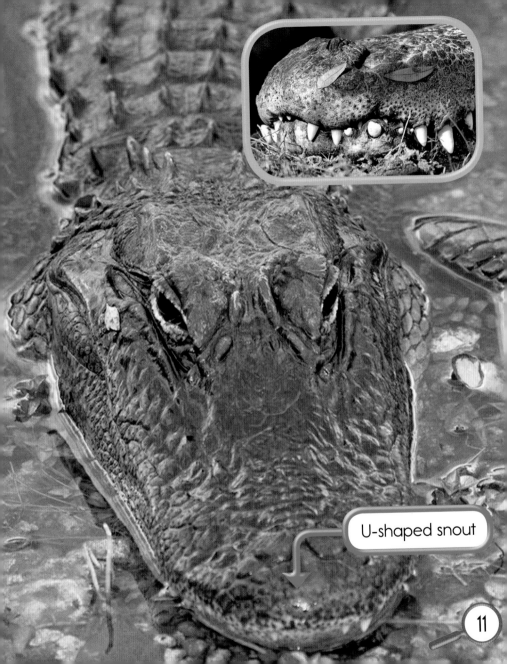

U-shaped snout

Killer Looks

Crocodiles and alligators have long, heavy bodies. Some can grow longer than cars! They also have four short legs. Both have hard scales that make their skin look bumpy.

A crocodile's skin is often dull green, gray, or brown.

This Nile crocodile lives in Africa.

Can you spot the alligator in this photo?

An alligator has darker skin than a crocodile. It may be dark green or even black. An alligator can look like a log floating in the water.

FUN FACT!

Crocodiles and alligators can stay underwater for up to two hours!

14

This alligator is waiting for its next meal to come by.

Mighty Hunters

Crocodiles and alligators eat meat. They hunt fish, birds, frogs, and turtles. They also eat deer, raccoons, and other big animals.

Crocodiles and alligators hunt in the same way. They poke just their eyes and nose above the water. Then they wait quietly until an animal comes near.

SNAP! Crocodiles and alligators quickly snatch their **prey**. They do not chew their food. They swallow the prey whole. If it is too big, they tear it into pieces.

This crocodile is hunting wildebeests.

Bringing Up Babies

Crocodiles and alligators start out in eggs.

Crocodile mothers dig a hole in the ground. They lay 30 to 70 eggs in the hole. Then they bury the eggs. After the little crocodiles hatch, their mother takes them to the water.

A baby crocodile pokes out of its egg.

An alligator makes a nest of twigs, mud, and plants. It looks like a big mound. She lays 20 to 50 eggs inside. The babies break through their shells. They ride in their mother's mouth or on her back to the water.

Now you know the difference between these animal look-alikes!

Right before they are about to hatch, baby alligators start to chirp.

A baby alligator gets
a ride from its mom.

Crocodiles and Alligators

Crocodiles and alligators live in warm places. Both crocodiles and alligators swim in freshwater. Crocodiles also swim in salt water._

North America

South America

MAP KEY

Alligator range

Crocodile range

Crocodiles and alligators live together in the wild in just one place. That is in southern Florida.

24

Europe

Asia

Africa

Australia

Antarctica

The Chinese alligator is rare. It lives in a small area of China.

Nile crocodiles live in Africa. Both parents guard the nest until their babies hatch.

What's the

crocodile

tough, scaly,
light-colored skin

top and bottom
teeth can be seen
when jaw is closed

long, pointed,
V-shaped snout

Meet the biggest crocodile that ever lived. Scientists found fossils of its bones in the Sahara desert. This monster was as long as a city bus. It even ate dinosaurs for dinner. No wonder experts have nicknamed it SuperCroc!

This picture shows what SuperCroc might have looked like.

Scientist Paul Sereno poses with the SuperCroc skull he discovered.

To figure out what SuperCroc looked like and how it acted, scientists pieced together the fossils they found. They added this information to what they know about crocodiles today. Super cool!

Guess Who?

- ✓ I have dark skin.
- ✓ My wide snout is shaped like the letter U.
- ✓ I build a nest made of mud, twigs, and plants.

Am I a crocodile or an alligator?

Answer: alligator.

Glossary

prey (PRAY): animal that is hunted by another animal for food

reptiles (REP-tiles): animals with lungs, scales, and backbones. Their body temperature is the same as that of the air around them.

scaly (SKAY-lee): covered in hard protective plates

snout (SNOWT): the long nose and mouth of an animal

Index

Facts for Now

Visit this Scholastic Web site for more information
on crocodiles and alligators:
www.factsfornow.scholastic.com
Enter the keywords **Crocodiles and Alligators**

About the Author

Lisa M. Herrington has written many books and articles about animals for kids. She lives in Trumbull, Connecticut, with her husband, Ryan, and daughter, Caroline.